THE GREAT
SOFTWARE HEIST

THE GREAT SOFTWARE HEIST

*Why everyone is paying too much to run
their software and what you can do about it*

STEVE BUTLER

First published in Britain in 2016

By Software Value Optimisation (www.softwarevalueoptimisation.com)

ISBN: 978-1541148161

DEDICATION

To Amanda for your patience

To Simon for your support and encouragement

And the many other people who have helped formulate
this approach over the last 10 years who are
too numerous to mention.

CONTENTS

1

INTRODUCTION

This book is about driving down the costs of IT and making enterprise applications more cost-effective.

It takes you on a journey.

That isn't for the faint-hearted. There is a lot of extremely worthwhile work involved which will yield many benefits for your organisation. One of my clients saved 25% of their IT budget, showing the potential rewards.

Almost all businesses can achieve a worthwhile savings by running through the Software Value Optimisation method described in this book.

1.1. The problem with software...

Although it is really straightforward to buy a software application, understanding the true costs of running one is much more difficult.

Most, if not all organisations struggle to understand the true costs, and as a result end up paying more for each service than they realise.

The associated environment to run modern software is becoming ever more complex, and it is not simple to understand all of the elements involved in delivering an application as a service to your organisation.

This book first looks at how to determine the costs of running each service and then how to reduce these costs.

It is possible to reduce the costs of existing applications as well as new applications. A number of examples are discussed later in the book.

The ultimate goal is to achieve a state where your environment is deliberately designed to reduce the costs of buying and running software.

I have called this approach **"Software Value Optimisation"** which contains 3 stages and 6 steps to reduce costs and improve the return on your investment.

1.2. Context

The method underpinning this book came out over many years working to deliver solutions that met my clients' needs, but perhaps more importantly, their budgets.

This approach has been further refined by finding ways to reduce the costs of maintaining large, legacy estates for major organisations. I have distilled this into a reusable approach that works across a broad range of industries.

My motivation for documenting this approach came from realising that some vendors have an unusual attitude towards their customers. Most of us operate on the basis that you provide value to your clients and take pride in doing a good job.

However, some in the software industry don't operate like this.

Can you imagine any other industry where your suppliers treat you like a potential criminal?

Their contracts are stuffed full of small print and weasel word clauses that give them the right to demand an audit and access your data centre at a moment's notice.

These "rights" enable them to treat you like some form of cash cow and demand extra money when it suits them.

Case study 1

I was working for one organisation where a vendor changed their terms and conditions with a set of patches for their product. This upgrade was installed, but it was not stated that these terms and conditions had changed.

The vendor then decided to demand more money from my client retrospectively even though they had had installed the licences in line with the vendor's recommendations.

When they objected, the vendor invoked their right to an audit to see if they could increase their potential revenue even further. The sums of money involved were over £10M. There was no basis to their claims and it was eventually sorted, but without an apology and incurring substantial legal fees in the process.

Not every software vendor behaves like this, but this is a true story and I can quote many others.

On the upside, these experiences provided me with insight into licencing models and the overall costs of deploying and maintaining software. These are explored in detail through this book.

One of the key insights is that there are many components and cost drivers in running software. With some thought, it is possible to identify the optimal solution for your needs, enabling costs to be reduced.

Cash Cows

There are vendors in the market who deliberately acquire other software products in order to build their portfolio of "Cash Cow" products.

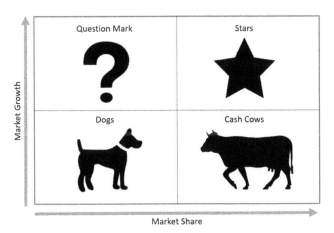

Their basic strategy is to find products with high revenues, steady demand, and needing minimal investment to maintain them. These products make the greatest amount of money for the vendor.

The annual support & maintenance fees for these products fund the vendor's profits, and if they are lucky they get away with little expenditure until the product is no longer needed by the market.

From my point of view, these annual fees for cash cow products provide the lowest value return for your investment. New releases only tend to be maintenance fixes and new functionality to add value is rare. Products in this category are often best avoided.

2

THE NEW SOLUTION

The fact is that the cost of deploying software is too high.

This book is an exploration of the real costs of running software and what you can do to reduce them.

First let's get into the nitty gritty of costs, benefits and return on investment.

Don't panic, this is not an accountancy course, just a recap of why we use software.

If you have written business cases to justify expenditure, then you are already familiar with Return on Investment (ROI).

There needs to be clear benefits for deploying software and the associated expense, time and effort.

Benefits are split into two distinct types:

- **Tangible.** Put simply, this is where running this software will provide measurable savings or even produce income.
- **Non-tangible.** Software can deliver other benefits that are not readily quantifiable. This can range from compliance with legislation and audit requirements through to enabling a team to better share documentation. Some of these may have financial benefits, but are difficult to establish or measure.

A business case will then assess these benefits against the implementation and running costs. There is then a value judgement to ensure that this investment makes sense.

One CFO I know worked on the basis that any investment had to make more than he would gain by leaving the money in a savings account. Others have required a payback period of typically 18 months.

Software costs are based on 5 main components:

- **Licence costs.** The vendor will make a charge to purchase or rent their software based upon the number of users, configuration, use, etc.
- **Implementation costs.** Every software package has a number of prerequisites including other software components, hardware, operating system and database. All of these need to be purchased, installed, configured and tested.
- **Running costs.** Keeping the software operational requires resources such as electricity, support, backups, monitoring and administration.
- **Lifecycle costs.** Few applications are static, they need periodic maintenance to stay operational and productive. Payroll systems have regular tax code updates, applications have patches, new versions and releases. Anti-virus systems need constant updates to stay effective. These go on for as long as the software is used.
- **Decommissioning costs.** At the end of its life, the application needs decommissioning and/or replacing. This includes the servers and the secure disposal of the data and disks.

A business case needs to take all of these factors into consideration to truly understand the costs of running software. However, the vast majority of business cases do not.

In reality, the purchase price of the software can be less than the running costs, particularly when you look over an extended period.

Example 1

Area	Component	Costs	Year 1	Year 2	Year 3	Year 4	Year 5	Year 6
Licence								
	CRM System		£ 100,000	£ 15,000	£ 15,000	£ 15,000	£ 15,000	£ 15,000
	Reporting tool							
Implementation								
	Project management		£ 50,000					
	Architect		£ 60,000					
	Developer		£ 45,000					
	Tester		£ 15,000					
	5 servers		£ 25,000	£ 5,000	£ 5,000	£ 5,000	£ 5,000	£ 5,000
Running								
	Electricity & aircon		£ 5,000	£ 5,000	£ 5,000	£ 5,000	£ 5,000	£ 5,000
	BAU Service		£ 25,000	£ 25,000	£ 25,000	£ 25,000	£ 25,000	£ 25,000
Lifecycle								
	Patching			£ 5,000	£ 5,000	£ 5,000	£ 5,000	£ 5,000
	Upgrade effort			£ 15,000	£ 15,000	£ 15,000	£ 15,000	£ 15,000
	Testing			£ 5,000	£ 5,000	£ 5,000	£ 5,000	£ 5,000
Decommission								
								£ 30,000
Annual Total			£ 325,000	£ 75,000	£ 75,000	£ 75,000	£ 75,000	£ 105,000
	Inflation Weighting			£ 76,500	£ 78,030	£ 79,591	£ 81,182	£ 82,806
Overall Total			£ 650,000	£ 150,000	£ 150,000	£ 150,000	£ 150,000	£ 210,000
6 year total			£ 1,460,000					

First impressions are that the licence and implementation costs would be the lion's share of the costs. However, the first-year cost of £650K is exceeded by the costs for the next five years of £810K.

Developing this lifecycle model is essential to understand the costs of running the key applications within your organisation. These costs are often referred to as Total Cost of Ownership (TCO).

Driving costs downwards

These are the 'low hanging fruit'. In example 1, the single greatest cost is the CRM system. The vendor-support charges are normally based upon a percentage of licence cost.

Cost-saving starts with procurement, but there are many other areas where these costs can be driven downwards. If you can drive down the licence costs, everything else drops as well. The chances are that your procurement team will get the best deal and in some sectors such as Government, there are standard prices for software.

Benefits

There is another approach to improving the ROI, namely increasing or better quantifying the benefits.

Let's say that a new mobile application deployed to a large sales force of a company was estimated to reduce their mileage by 1,000,000 miles annually. At 30 miles per gallon, this would equate to a saving of 33,333 gallons a year. Fuel prices fluctuate, but at £5 per gallon, this would give a saving of £160K per year.

As many savings can be difficult to prove, most business cases tend to be conservative and avoid committing to anything difficult to measure. However, it is quite possible that more benefits have been delivered than originally stated. It is well worth revisiting these to see if anything has been missed.

Exercise

Find a business case relating to a significant software application within your business.

Take a look through this to understand how your organisation measures the costs and benefits.

What are the criteria to justify the expenditure? Was it based on a simple measure of ROI? How was the project going to prove the benefits were realised?

Understanding these will help to see what you need to do in order to deliver savings.

Summary

ROI is the tangible benefits minus the total cost over a period of time.

Return = (Benefits – costs) / Time

Increasing the benefits or decreasing the costs improves the ROI.

The rest of this book looks at the software costs and opportunities to reduce these in much more detail.

I have developed a scorecard to help identify cost-saving opportunities and highlight potential risks. This can be found at

http://softwarevalueoptimisation.com/software-scorecard-2/

3
SOFTWARE IS THE SUM OF ITS PARTS

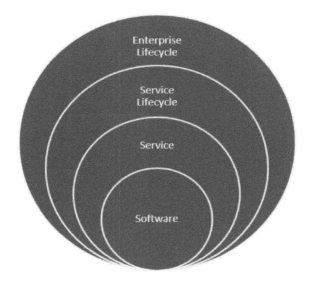

In the last 20 years, there has been explosive change in the role that software plays in our work and home lives. Many roles simply wouldn't be possible without the use of specialised software.

As an example, most people spend some time every day checking their emails or browsing the web.

Software has literally taken over.

We have also seen a whole new set of challenges that come with this software explosion.

As some applications have become Mission Critical, we need better ways of monitoring and managing these.

As a part of this evolution, there are several trends changing the way that we manage software.

- **Few users to Thousands of users.** Software is no longer installed to just a single PC. It is often installed onto thousands of machines. Loading the software has become a project in its own right. Supporting thousands of users also presents a new set of challenges.
- **Few parts to many parts.** The application is no longer stand-alone; it also requires many other components to work. All of these components have to be at specific versions to work with the application.
- **Applications to services.** Once installed, an application needs to be supported and maintained. It has evolved to become a service. It may have a service-level agreement defining the hours of support, support mechanisms and many other details of the service. This also implies a team able to support this service along with the associated costs.

Delivering services is much more complex than installing a simple application, but also delivers considerable benefits to an organisation, especially where the service is critical to their operation.

In order to understand the costs of delivering applications as a service, let's have a look at some of the fundamental concepts behind these.

3.1. Stacks — The software Russian Doll

In the good old days, we just talked about applications and gave little thought to how they ran.

Today's applications are far more complex beasts. Some applications need dozens of extra components to work properly.

Engineering has wrestled with this complexity for many years. Take a car; it is made from something like 10,000 parts. Many of these are grouped in assemblies, serving a particular function such as braking.

Building the Apollo rockets was so complicated that NASA worked with IBM to create the first Database called IMS helping them manage the vast number of parts and associated bill of materials.

A software package is merely the tip of the iceberg. Understanding all of the components needed to run an application is key to understanding its true cost to your organisation.

Software Value Optimisation defines three specific groups containing these components:

- **Software Stack**.
- **Application Stack**.
- **Service Stack**.

Let's have a look at each of these in more detail.

3.2. The Software Stack

Few applications are truly standalone. Developing modern applications depends upon a variety of third-party components and tools to speed up development and make it easier to support a wide variety of platforms.

When you install a basic application on a PC, it unpacks a range of components and then proceeds to install these on your PC or server. It's often surprising just how many elements get installed.

These modules often cover areas such as:

- Programming language run times such as C++ or Java
- Productivity tools such as frameworks
- User interface
- License managers

Many applications bundle everything together using special tools and the installation package is the resulting bundle containing everything needed. Often you will also have to install other third-party prerequisites before you install your software.

There are many problems that occur due to these extra components. Servers frequently run more than one application and these systems may use the same files or components, but with differing versions. Often, the only way to tell which version you have is to check the file size.

Applications will only work reliably with the correct version. This condition has been called "DLL Hell" and has caused many problems in environments such as Citrix.

This subject is explored in more detail in the chapter on Managing the Software Lifecycle.

In order to understand how to reduce costs effectively, it is important that all elements of an application are understood.

3.3. The Application Stack

This stack includes everything needed to run the application and its associated software stack.

Let's have a look at the most common elements of this:

- **Data interfaces**. Your application may use Oracle, SQL Server, MySQL or a wide range of drivers to access local or networked databases.
- **Middleware.** This is typically for items such as Service-Orientated Architecture (SOA), web services such as Apache and Web brokers. These elements are used to simplify and standardise access to features such as data and web resources.
- **Management tools.** Data Centres with more than a few servers or PCs run specific tools to help them manage their estate. This can range from Anti-Virus software through to software distribution such as Microsoft's SCCM, licensing and asset management software.
- **Operating system (OS).** Every application runs on some form of OS from an embedded appliance through to Windows, UNIX and Apple servers. There are also many different OS editions and licence types. As the size of a data centre grows, it can be advantageous to use different licence types. This can reduce management overheads and costs.
- **Hypervisors or virtualisation tools**. Modern virtualisation tools such as VMware, XenApp and HyperV have enabled underutilised servers to be better exploited by enabling many virtual servers to be run from a single physical server. However, it is necessary to understand which hypervisor software is deployed as there can be hidden costs and licencing issues. Some vendors try to increase their charges depending on your virtual infrastructure. Understanding this helps to avoid these costs.
- **Hardware.** The application runs on either dedicated server(s) or virtual machines. A Configuration Management Database (CMDB) should record this information.
- **Storage.** The server OS, application files and database reside on some form of disk whether it is cloud storage, local hard disks or a Storage Area Network (SAN). Backups also need some form of storage. Each of these components has associated costs. It may also need specialised storage drivers to access SANs or network drives by methods that are not included within the OS.
- **Networks.** Finally, the servers are accessed via the local & wide area networks or even the Internet. Depending on the route, there may be widely varying charges and even penalties associated with excessive use.

Exercise

Take a major application and see how many of the stack components you can identify.

Use the labels given in this section and record any components
found against each of the labels.

It is worth adding up the total number of components to get an
idea of the complexity of the software.

3.4. Service Stack

The Service Stack is a new concept which recognises that the application
stack delivers a service to your business, clients and colleagues. This
service needs to be clearly understood as it impacts the delivery costs
and even how the associated infrastructure is designed.

A service level agreement (SLA) defines a service, its performance and
how it is measured. It should also identify who is responsible for delivering support.

Often more than one party can be responsible. There may be an internal
service desk that provides the first-line support, but ultimately backs this
off to a third party. The product vendor may also be involved.

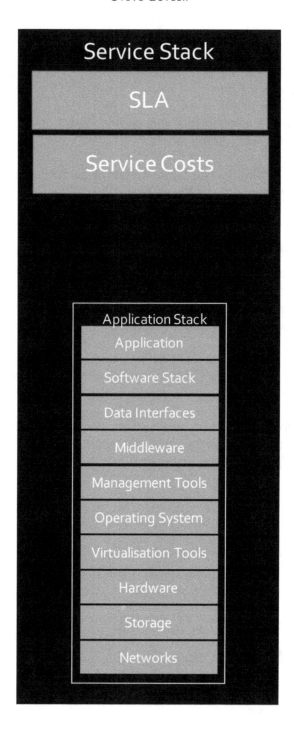

3.5. Service Level Agreement (SLA) Definition

An SLA is a formal guarantee of a service being delivered. It usually involves 2 parties: the provider and the receiver or client. It describes the service in terms of the scope, the quality and responsibilities of the parties to the agreement.

There should be a number of Key Performance Indicators (KPIs) that allow the performance of the service to be judged.

The key to this is a measure of the performance of the service, i.e., how you measure that this is being delivered according to the quality measures in the SLA and that the anticipated benefits are being realised.

There may be penalties for non-performance, often in the form of service credits. However, the goal of both parties is to avoid the service getting to the point where the quality standards have been breached.

Another control in an SLA should define the mean time between failures (MTBF). This is a measure of the reliability of the service. The other key measure is mean time to repair (MTTR). This defines how long it will take to get the service working again after a failure.

Service Costs

Each service has an overall cost that comprises the application stack elements, plus the service management components needed to manage and monitor the service.

Exercise

Using the application that you identified in the previous exercise, now add in the SLA details such as the hours of service, recovery time, planned downtime, etc.

If possible, look at the BAU budget allocated to this service.

Also look at the benefits identified in the business case and look to see how these are being measured.

3.6. Summary

The cost of running an application is much higher than it first appears. The cost of the application, its associated application stack and software stack, as well as the service stack need to be included to understand the whole cost.

Conversely, removing or reducing these elements enables these costs to be reduced and in turn increases the ROI.

4

SOFTWARE VALUE OPTIMISATION – A SIX-STEP MODEL

I like to refer to this as the six pillars.

Each one of these is part of the way in which costs can be understood and reduced. Individually they are all important, but when combined they become more than the sum of their parts.

Let's look at each of these in turn.

4.1. The First Pillar – Discovery

"Know yourself and know your enemy
and you will win every time."
Sun Tzu - "The Art of War".

The discovery pillar is about understanding your applications and the associated stacks. Given this information, you can make informed decisions and find savings. Without this, it is extremely difficult to progress.

There are a number of ways in which this data can be captured. ITIL refers to the Configuration Management Database (CMDB). It is sometimes referred to as a Master Application List (MAL).

Some organisations have gathered this in spreadsheets.

Keeping accurate and comprehensive records is a time-consuming task. However, it is essential to ensure software compliance which is discussed in later chapters.

These records can be collected and maintained via a manual or automated process or a mixture of the two. Please note that licence reconciliation requires manual input.

Key Point

In my experience, 90% of the problems in maintaining applications, application audits and data centre migrations result from incomplete records. Even more so if you are looking to outsource, where incomplete data will result in additional charges and delays.

"Asset management tools are not optional.
They are the only sane way to maintain the quality
of records to support a sizeable IT function"

Exercise

Identify how your organisation records the details of all of its services. Is there a CMDB or Master Application List?

Familiarise yourself with this to see how much detail is recorded against each of the services.

How was this information collated? Was it manually or were automation tools used? If there were tools, try and find out what they were.

Do these lists go beyond basic application details and record the service stack information?

Are any details kept of the software costs and the maintenance costs within these lists?

If not, pick a couple of the applications and look up the pricing on Amazon or a price-comparison site. Assume that the maintenance cost is 15% of the purchase price per year.

4.2. The Second Pillar – Tuning Your Infrastructure

Most of us inherited the IT infrastructure that our services run on. IT over the last 30 years has exploded haphazardly with little thought about how it could best be optimised.

This legacy infrastructure has consequently driven how applications are installed and their associated costs.

There is a golden opportunity to turn this on its head and design your infrastructure to reduce running costs.

Servers.

Many licencing models are based upon the number of processor cores or memory. The greater a server's resources, the more you were billed.

Virtualisation has radically changed this charging model. Going back 10 years ago, new applications were typically designed with dedicated servers. Although simpler from a design perspective, these servers were rarely more than 10% loaded.

The founders of VMware realised that it would be possible to use this spare capacity by allowing a single physical server to hold many virtual servers. Effectively, this single server could now run 10 or more of these virtual servers utilising the spare capacity. At a stroke, this revolutionised the server industry and dramatically reduced the costs of deploying applications. These virtual servers are called "Virtual Machines" or a VM.

Several years ago, there was an outcry when VMware suddenly decided to move to a memory -based model.

Virtualisation's bottleneck was always around having sufficient memory. If you had enough you could increase the number of lightly loaded Virtual Machines (VM) that you could run on each physical host.

Twice the memory equated to double the number of VM halving your cost. VMware's charges were based upon the number of physical servers. By linking their licences to the memory size as well, VMware effectively doubled their charges overnight.

The resulting outcry eventually sunk this charging model.

Many CIOs were suddenly looking at shifting to Microsoft's Hyper-V, VMware's main competitor, as it suddenly looked very attractive, especially as VMs can easily be moved between different vendor's virtualisation products.

However, virtualisation technologies present many opportunities to tune the infrastructure to minimise licence costs.

A good example of exploiting this flexibility is where a vendor bases their pricing model upon a physical measure such as memory or CPU cores.

A VM looks identical to a physical server and its configuration can be adjusted from the management tools. Simply reducing memory or cores so that there is enough to run the app allows your charges to be minimised!

There are other tricks that can be applied. Even if you reduce the number of processor cores available to a VM, you can still actually increase the speed of the available cores.

The clock speed of the core is measured in MHz or GHz. It is possible to increase the speed to create a more powerful VM. If your original VM had 2 cores running at 1GHz each, you could assign a single core, but increase its MHz to 2GHZ so that overall, the VM still had the same horsepower.

VMware and other tools enable you to create virtual processors which combine a number of physical processors allowing you to create servers more powerful than any individual processor. They also allow fractions of physical processors to be assigned. This allows the VM to be sized for its workload and minimises the licencing costs.

The great thing is that this can be done by VM so that you can tune this for each service in your organisation. Optimising your VMs according to the licencing restrictions of each vendor gives a lot of scope to keep costs down.

It is worth saying that some optimisation of the virtual infrastructure may be needed once you have built the VMs to deal with your more difficult applications. A good administrator will have the tools and skills for this.

Exercise

If you are running VMware or Hyper-V, use the admin tools to report on the resource allocation for a couple of the applications used in the previous exercises.

Look for the processor cycles, cores and memory allocation. Then look for the utilisation figures. Would it be possible to allocate less without taking the utilisation too close to the limit?

Storage

Modern servers make extensive use of a Storage Area Network (SAN) and Flash storage. Many servers only come with Flash boot drives these

23

days as it radically increases reliability and decreases boot times over mechanical drives.

A tiered storage architecture provides a mixture of fast, slow and backup / archive technologies to meet the varying demands of applications. Databases typically need the fastest storage, whilst non-critical applications can get away with slower and cheaper technologies such as SATA drives.

However, collectively, storage is very expensive. Also, as performance increases, the prices tend to rise very quickly.

It is not only the storage, but also the mechanisms used to connect servers to storage. Using an Ethernet network running over Gigabit Ethernet or faster is the default way to connect to this storage. However, the highest performance requires Fibre or optical connections. The Fibre infrastructure is dramatically more expensive than Ethernet, adding considerably to the cost of storage.

In the software stack, understanding the storage volumes, types and connections is critical.

Outsourcing contracts tend to be very expensive in terms of the storage fees. There will be a price per GB for the different types of storage. This fee should include the backup and restore of the data as well.

A few years ago, I had a very interesting discussion with a CEO. We needed an extra 4Tb of storage and the outsourcer wanted around £20K for this per year! These prices had been established at the start of an outsourcing contract and no longer reflected current market rates.

The CEO came back with an interesting response "I just bought a 1TB drive from PC World at the weekend and it cost me £100. Why on earth are we paying 20 grand a year for this!"

The conversation was actually a lot more colourful, but you can see where they were coming from.

Cloud computing has opened up some innovative ways to reduce your storage costs. Both Amazon and Microsoft's Cloud models have fixed prices for storage. These prices vary slightly depending on the services being purchased, but they are extremely cheap relative to traditional outsourcers.

A great example is Microsoft's Office 365. Have you ever been fed up with running out of space in your inbox every couple of weeks?

Office 365 has up to 1Tb of storage per user and removes a tedious and time-consuming drudge of having to clean up your inbox all of the time. Having to clean up your inbox on a weekly basis uses a lot of time over a year. It is a false economy to offer small inboxes as any marginal saving on storage is soon wasted on the productivity reductions multiplied across your staff.

Running an in-house Exchange email system which uses SAN storage quickly becomes a very expensive option. If you have 5000 users each with 200GB of storage, this gives a total of 1000TB of storage. With an old outsourcing contract, this could easily have cost hundreds of thousands of pounds each year!

Many email systems will pay for themselves in terms of the storage costs alone. As an example, Office 365 currently costs £10 per month per user. I have seen a number of business cases where Office 365 has reduced the costs by between 50% and 75% over an outsourced solution.

Networks

How do your users access their applications?

Network bandwidth is not free. How these services are accessed also contributes to the costs.

If you are moving to a cloud model, there may be more load on your internet connections. This may require a bandwidth upgrade. Upgrades are incremental and require you to go up to the next size moving from 1 Gbps to 2 Gbps, for example. These incremental costs are significant and must be costed.

Other options also include upgrading your dedicated data centre links and WAN links to individual offices. The bandwidth requirements depend on the nature of the application and the traffic flows. Often, a pilot is the only way to accurately estimate these costs.

4.3. The Third Pillar - Selecting the best licencing models

*Licencing is far more than just purchasing
a licence or right to use a vendor's software.*

*Understanding the licence types available and which best suits
your needs can reduce your deployment costs by 4 to 1 or more*

Software products are typically offered with a variety of different licence types. These models offer considerable potential to match your environment and requirements to the most suitable means of deploying the software.

It is not unusual for there to be a 50% cost reduction or more resulting from selecting the most appropriate model. A good example is database software where there are a variety of models available. These are often based upon a per-user or per-core basis. Depending on your environment, there can be a substantial cost difference between the two models.

Software tends to fall into one of two types: Leased or Purchased. Leased is where you have to pay a periodic fee to the Software vendor. Purchased is where you have bought a licence to use that particular version indefinitely.

This is sometimes referred to as **"Perpetual"**.

Perpetual is by far the most common and traditional model. This basically means that you own a given number of copies of the software and can continue to use this for as long as needed.

There are a number of significant variations to the perpetual model:

- **Perpetual plus limited upgrades.** This licence includes a fixed number of versions, releases or patches. Typically, you purchase 1 or 3 years of upgrades. It normally includes maintenance and lets you contact the vendors support service.
- **Perpetual plus annual maintenance.** In this model, there is an annual charge which entitles you to support and upgrades. The fee for this is typically 15%, although some vendors try to push this higher.

Other licence types

- **Lease.** This model has a periodic charge for use of the software. This is typically monthly or annually, although there are also other intervals such as quarterly and half yearly. An excellent example of this is Office 365 which provides web versions of the Office applications, online email and storage as well as the right to use the full versions on desktop and laptop PCs.
- **Per use.** This model charges you each time the software is used. The charges can also vary depending on the quantities of data processed. This applies mostly to online services. Print on Demand services are a good example of this model.
- **Freeware.** This type of software is free of any charges, although this may not be the case for commercial use. There are often caveats so it is worth checking carefully.
- **Shareware.** This type of software can be free, but often there is a voluntary donation if the software is useful or certain features only work if you pay for an upgrade.
- **General Public Licence.** This is an industry standard for free software that allows running, studying, sharing and modification.
- **Bespoke.** This customises the contract for each client. This normally applies to expensive enterprise software and carries high legal costs and lengthy negotiation periods.

The standard End User Licence Agreement (EULA) is by far the most popular. This is often referred to as a Shrink Wrap license as the vendor only supplies it if you agree to certain terms. By opening the package and installing the software, you are deemed to have accepted the terms and conditions.

These conditions are often biased in favour of the vendor and should be checked if you are buying lots of copies of the application.

It is worth noting that software normally contains clauses that state that the vendor does not warrant the software to be free of defects or make any commitment to fix these defects. It also excludes suitability for purpose, meaning there are no guarantees that it will be right for your circumstances.

These are fairly standard clauses and are best tackled by piloting applications before committing to large-scale deployments.

4.4. The Fourth Pillar – Understand your Utilisation

How software is used within your organisation is the key to determining which licence type will be the cheapest.

Case Study

An organisation used an IBM mainframe for several of its key business applications. Initially, almost every employee in the organisation used this software. However, the business had moved in a new system and to a PC-based platform. The mainframe service was retained, but its usage was dramatically reduced.

This system was accessed via another vendor's terminal emulator package running on a PC. An enterprise license had been purchased which entitled all staff to use this emulator and the annual maintenance contract was for over 1500 staff.

A conservative estimate showed that a maximum of 100 people now needed access and probably less than 50.

Looking at this utilisation figure, it made no sense to continue with the enterprise license. The vendor offered a concurrent licence allowing a maximum number of people to use the software at a time.

The software was purchased and the licencing components were put in place to measure the usage.

This simple change resulted in a £100K saving per year, a very significant outcome.

Understanding utilisation enables you to choose the most appropriate licencing mechanism, and it can make dramatic reductions in the maintenance charges.

In the case study above, it was fairly straightforward to determine the usage and then work out the best licensing model.

In some cases, it can be more complex to understand usage.

There are two useful tools that can help better understand utilisation:

- **Software Asset management.** This is a category of software tools used to determine the software running on PCs and servers. These can find the installed software and provide information on its usage. The reporting tools enable this to be aggregated so that summary information can be provided showing the use by application over time.
- **Citrix or terminal services.** Citrix has similar reporting capabilities built into the console. If you are delivering applications via Citrix, there can be many opportunities to use more beneficial licence types. Logging needs to be enabled to collect this information.

Exercise

Take a look at the larger applications used within your organisation. Can you identify which types of licence models they use?

4.5. The Fifth Pillar – Refine your support model

The service stack is a wrapper around the application stack providing support and maintenance. This is typically provided in-house or via a third-party services defined via an SLA and a service contract.

The SLA requirements in terms of response times and recovery points drive the costs of this service.

A simple break fix service with no formal recovery time tends to be fairly inexpensive, but gives you the least contractual leverage to protect your services.

A "Gold" service on the other hand, is considerably more expensive due to its higher levels of service availability and the additional resource needed to deliver this.

There are several models in common use for defining these services:

- Service Wrapper
- Operational Level Agreement (OLA)
- SLA

The Service Wrapper is the most basic giving the lowest level of service and effectively a "Gentleman's agreement" to try and hit the target service levels. There is no commercial penalty for not hitting them.

The OLA is more rigorous than the service wrapper and would tend to have many of the targets and measurements of an SLA, but without any penalties for non-compliance.

The SLA is the most robust incorporating targets, measurements and penalties. It's like an OLA but with teeth. Penalties normally take the form of service credits, but can also be financial penalties.

Although this penalty mechanism gives reassurance that the service will be delivered to a high standard, the relationship between the client and the vendor has often broken down by the time that these are being claimed. A competent vendor would seek to fix the situation long before it reached this point.

Each of these models balance guaranteed service levels against cost. The charges reflect the resourcing and the degree of risk to the provider.

This is probably the main area within outsourcing contracts that generates friction and bad feeling.

As an example, SLAs struggle around software upgrades. Most outsourcers will only freely upgrade where there has been no change to the functionality of the package. If there are new features, they will almost always expect to charge extra to cover development costs and, of course, their profit margin.

Most clients on the other hand expect that upgrades are free and part of the SLA. I believe that 99% of all outsourcing contracts run into this trap and it causes a lot of friction. Handling of upgrades and patching should be defined as a part of the SLA so that there is no ambiguity.

If an in-house team was supporting an application, they would have to pick up the support of any new functionality in later versions and releases without increasing headcount.

Outsourcers on the other hand, will try and avoid this. An upgrade necessitates upgrading test plans and then checking these each time the software is upgraded.

An SLA should include this as an obligation for the provider for the duration of the contract.

Another related trap is that outsourcers often do not include any effort or obligation to upgrade the software. It is often relegated to a customer-driven and chargeable change request.

The problem is that the SLA does not mention upgrades and it gets assumed that the outsourcer will do this as the in-house team would have done. The problems then arise when it is discovered that this is not covered and has also not been budgeted. This is another of the areas where outsourcing contracts cost more than anticipated.

An SLA should either explicitly include upgrades or state that they are not covered.

There are a number of terms commonly used in delivering support:

- **First-line support.** This is where the outsourcer provides a service desk or help desk support service. Most problems get resolved at this point. However, some require more expert assistance.
- **Second and third-line support.** These provide more technical and product-specific knowledge to resolve problems. Occasionally, they will also liaise with the application vendor where a problem is a bug or there is no obvious explanation.

Most outsourced service desks will insist on having active vendor support in place so that bugs and complex technical issues can be resolved. An outsourcing generalist rarely has the same level of expertise as the vendor.

The IT Industry seems to swing between extremes. About 10 years ago, the fashion was to use the large outsourcers to take over many of your services and run these on your behalf.

Currently, the pendulum seems to be swinging back to using smaller specialist partners. These are often far better to work with and have true skills in their specialties.

Large outsourcers tend to have much higher charges than your internal rates making them very expensive. If you are outsourcing to save money, the combination of higher charges and hidden extras means it rarely saves money in reality.

Outsourcers are mostly generalists. If you want advice and consultancy, they rarely have expert skills in this area. Deep skills require a specialist or boutique consultancy.

A different skillset is needed to manage multiple vendors. This can result in deploying tools and standardising processes (and measurement) across all your vendors. There are costs embedded with this approach as you need to manage more partners. This typically means having service managers and a product such as Service Now, which is rapidly become a *de facto* tool in this space.

These costs can become lost in operational budgets, but need to be understood in order to establish the true cost of running each service.

Accountants have tools for evaluating these costs, called **Activity-Based Costing**. Looking at a service in isolation, it is easy to miss the overheads of managing a range of vendors.

Most calculations will understate the real cost and it becomes easy to make poor decisions based on these erroneous costs. It's a bit like the organisational flattening trend of the 90s which obsessed with removing middle managers. Most of the time this simply moved critical tasks to other staff and reduced productivity, the exact opposite of what was intended.

The final element of the equation is **Compliance** and **Opportunity Costs.**

For fee earning and income-generating services, any downtime can result in reduced revenues and raised tempers. If these costs can be calculated, you have a tool to determine how much resilience is needed and indeed if it is justified. Spending £1M to save £100K per year is not a good investment!

It is also possible that there may be fines and penalties for services not being available. Cost avoidance needs to be considered and evaluated for each of these.

Many CFOs will use opportunity cost as a measure to evaluate investment. This may be dressed up as ROI or other similar measures, but they are basically asking if they could get a better return by investing the same money elsewhere.

These measures can be applied to existing systems as well as new to see if there are any other opportunities for saving money.

Exercise

Using the same applications, what type of agreements do you have in place?

Are the risks for each of these services clearly defined? Are the service levels clearly justified by the risks?

Can you see any opportunities to reduce these costs? Is there another way of running the service with lower day rates?

If you are using third parties, could you bring this in-house or bring a number of services in-house to reduce costs?

4.6. The Sixth Pillar – Find better substitutes

There are probably several if not dozens of ways to deliver the functionality of any given application.

With a bit of legwork, many alternatives can be found that reduce your running costs.

Marketing strategy provides two different concepts; that of substitutes and alternatives.

Substitutes

These are different products that do the same or a similar job. Substitutes are products that can easily be swapped with existing products.

The emphasis is normally on cost, and these do the same function for less money. They are effectively consumables. If you were buying a new car, you would normally go for the best deal. Software is becoming the same.

A great example of this is Adobe Reader and Writer. Reader lets you read PDF files, whilst writer lets you create these from a variety of common file formats.

Adobe's policy has been to offer Reader for free in order to become the *de facto* standard for portable documents. The downside is that Writer is expensive and often overly complex for creating simple documents.

For many organisations, the challenge has been to find cheaper ways of creating PDFs. Over time there has been a flow of useful tools that deliver most of this functionality at a lower cost. Some even are free.

Programs such as Microsoft Word will create PDFs. There are also many freeware and shareware products with varying features and support.

The same principle goes for many modern software tools.

Back in the 1990s Gorilla Marketing become well known as a marketing strategy for software companies, although it is by no means limited to them.

An organisation's marketing strategy could be divided into one of three levels:

- **The Gorilla.** This is where you are the biggest player in the market and banging your chest about being the best. It goes without saying that this player will be very expensive with complex deployment, high running costs and a diva-type personality. Know any of these?
- **The Orang-utan.** This vendor basically provides much of the functionality of the Gorilla's software, but at a lower price point. They're 'good enough'.
- **The Chimp.** This is typically a new entrant with a light weight version of the product that does the core functions well, but cheaply. Everything is focused on being cheaper and more agile.

If you are using enterprise-level software products, there will almost definitely be Orangutan and Chimp products in the market as well.

Alternatives

There are often more radical alternatives which may give similar results but via a very different route.

A radical form of this is process outsourcing. Most enterprise software tends to implement some form of business process. However, this can be enormously expensive due to the costs of the software and customisation costs.

Some services such as Amazon's Mechanical Turks allow tasks to be allocated to a large number of commodity workers for a very low cost.

So instead of just trying to make an existing package cheaper to run, you could outsource the entire business process to an outsourcer or an Amazon-type service using commodity resources and paying per transaction.

For some businesses this is incredibly disruptive and will further fuel automation and offshoring / right sourcing.

Further details can be found at: https://www.mturk.com/mturk/welcome

Identifying alternatives and substitutes

This comes down to a few straightforward steps.

Are there Shareware and Freeware alternatives?

If you are running a Gorilla product, what are the Chimps and Orangutans?

Can you code something which will deliver just what you need and avoid vendor fees?

Can you deliver the functionality via Cloud Services? Some IT functionality such as data cubes can be very expensive to maintain in-house and putting this out to Microsoft's Azure or Amazon Web Services can have a considerably lower cost, is scalable and has no long-term commitment.

Another example is in online publication production.

Print images are by their nature very high-quality and have very large file sizes.

For a digital publication or website these images need to be compressed to reduce their sizes. This is frequently done by hand using various tools that maximise the quality of the compressed images.

There are some file formats that compress, but the results are not always good enough for professional publications. There are now online compression services which use the most appropriate algorithms to get the best results, but are run as a batch process. You send hundreds of images across and they come back in the right form automatically.

Note: Always consider security when evaluating options.

As organisations become more careful about sensitive information, this must be factored into any decisions about alternatives and substitutes. Online services may operate outside of your country and their security standards may be different or even unacceptable.

The data classification needs to be understood as a part of this exercise.

Practical Exercise

- Identify your top 10 applications and run an internet search for each of these "Your Product Name" Alternative. You can also try searching your application name and replacement.
- If your organisation runs Enterprise software with a license for the whole organisation, are there other products in these bundles that might replace other paid applications?
- Have a look at some of the Shareware directories. https://sourceforge.net/ has an astonishing broad set of applications. Many chargeable utilities can be replaced with tools from this site. There are some very interesting Gorilla alternative tools here as well.

4.7. Summary

The 6 pillars are underpinned by the first pillar, Discovery. Once this is completed, the other 5 pillars provide opportunities to reduce your costs and often simplify delivery.

As a yardstick, I would expect that it should be possible to reduce the software budget by at least 10% using this approach.

To help simplify the process of reducing costs, I created the Software Value Optimisation Scorecard. This can be found at:

http://softwarevalueoptimisation.com/software-scorecard-2/

5

THE LIFECYCLE MODEL

All services have their own lifecycles and there are different costs associated with each of these stages. Understanding these stages enables effective planning which will reduce medium and long-term costs.

5.1. Service Lifecycle

Software follows the lifecycle models found in marketing. There are 5 stages in the life of a service:

- **Commission.** This is the process of introducing a new service into an organisation after it has been justified via a business case. This will build all of the prerequisite stack and set up the application. It will normally include training, documentation, service introduction and user access.

- **Maintain.** Services are not static - there is an ongoing require-ment to apply patches and perform basic configuration updates to keep the service working optimally. These are generally fairly small changes, but they are essential.
- **Upgrade.** At some point, it becomes necessary to upgrade the stacks to maintain vendor support, operation or security. This is a significant exercise and requires planning and testing. This is likely to happen a number of times during the lifetime of the service.
- **Replace.** Eventually, the service will be replaced by an alternative. Sometimes, there is no ongoing need for the application and it is simply decommissioned.
- **Decommission.** Once a service is either replaced or not required, the components need to be removed to prevent further charges. This includes secure disposal of data so that personal or sen-sitive information is properly erased.

These elements should be documented or at least considered as a part of the service documentation. They help to plan how the service is managed.

The maintain stage is the most reactive part of the lifecycle. Patches can be released by the application, database and OS vendors relatively randomly as they discover significant bugs or security vulnerabilities. Critical patches can be pushed out with no warning and need to be acted upon quickly.

Some vendors maintain periodic patch releases, e.g. every quarter. These are easier to manage and may be essential for areas such as financial systems.

The Upgrade stage is much more predictable and vendors publish time-lines for their products which makes planning straightforward.

The industry uses a number of key terms that help drive this planning process:

- **Versions** are the major updates of a product when they introduce significant new features. This introduces major changes from previous versions and requires a lot of effort to thoroughly test the service working closely with the users.

- **Releases** are minor updates and often fix many bugs. These still need testing, but not as extensively as a new version.

The formal "Version.Release" syntax is widely used to track the product level. For example, 1.3 would signify version 1, release 3.

It is worth saying that patches can be pushed out as new releases or sometimes as a sub release number such as 1.3.2.

A vendor will only support a version of a product for a fixed amount of time. It is extremely difficult and expensive for vendors to support lots of clients running older versions and releases of an application.

Therefore, vendors actively encourage their clients to upgrade to the latest or at least a recent version. There are two industry terms that relate to this support period.

- **End of Service (EOS).** This is a date after which the vendor will only offer limited support for a given version and release. After this point, they typically offer critical security fixes only. Some vendors such as Microsoft offer chargeable extended support. This is charged at a premium rate. There are often caveats around this such as not guarantying fixes and it may not offer the same SLA as the full support.
- **End of Life (EOL).** This is the point where no support at all is offered for this version & release. The vendor's response to any support calls will be to say that the product must be upgraded to a supported version.

Some vendors increase maintenance charges for older software to encourage their customers to move to later versions.

The individual service stack now needs to be set in the context of how long a vendor will provide support for a particular version and release of their software.

In any given year, there can be hundreds or even thousands of components approaching their end of support. The EOS/EOL needs to be recorded against each component.

However, in order to effectively manage the lifecycle, the EOS / EOL need to be set in the context of a 4 or 5-year window.

This enables management of work, budget and resources that are needed to facilitate these upgrades. With larger organisations, this is a major undertaking requiring a team to plan this work and potentially multiple teams to manage the upgrades. It also never stops. There will always be components requiring upgrades.

Exercise

Using the same applications as for the previous exercise, find out the vendor's published EOS/EOL for these applications.

If necessary, ring up the vendor to get these details.

How much time is there before any of these need to be upgraded?

5.2. The Real Lifecycle Cost

The cost of running software is much higher than is initially obvious.

Many financial models simply look at the deployment cost and the yearly maintenance costs

However, this overlooks that all of these elements have shelf lives and will need to be maintained. It is only when the lifecycle model is factored in that a true understanding of the cost be made.

Software Value Optimisation is a process that looks at an individual service, their underlying components and well as the bigger picture.

Although services tend to be planned individually, in reality these services overlap and interact with each other.

For many organisations, being unsupported is simply not an option. If the product is in widespread use or critical, then the risk is often too high.

A business's appetite for risk can determine whether a product should always be in vendor support. Some products such as Microsoft Office may not need to be supported as bugs may never be fixed. Whereas a bug in a billing system could delay or stop invoicing which is a far more serious situation.

Therefore, support decisions should be based upon the value to an organisation.

The Support Trade-off

Decisions about keeping applications in vendor support can have wide ranging consequences.

The annual fee is typically 15%. This can be a tempting target to save some money in the annual budgeting dance.

One company I worked with nearly came unstuck with this.

Case study 2

The client had deliberately decided that they no longer needed support for a legacy reporting package. It was about 4 years out of support and was being replaced by another vendor's enterprise software.

As a short-term measure, all of the current applications were being virtualised and migrated to a new data centre. The existing package would not virtualise successfully and it became necessary to upgrade the package so that it could be moved prior to its replacement.

A quick call to the vendor in question produced a quotation. Now you might have expected a simple fee for getting the next version and maybe having to get support for 12 months.

Potentially, even the sales person would be happy at the prospect of getting a bit more commission for an inactive customer.

However, in this case, they were feeling far more ambitious.

The quotation took up several pages which should have been a warning in itself....

First was the upgrade fee. A nice hefty fee for a lightly used product.

Then there was the fee for 12 months' support which was compulsory.

But they hadn't finished yet.

Then you had to purchase support for the 4 years that you had not been in support.... Yes, really!

And then there was a penalty, sorry I meant admin fee.... For the vendor agreeing to upgrade the software. And this wasn't small either.

The whole thing came to almost £200K which was probably more than the software had cost in the first place.

You can imagine the interesting conversation that came up with the IT Director and CFO. It was probably a good thing for the vendor that this quotation never made into the pages of Computer Weekly as this would have pretty much stopped them getting any more clients ever again.

Needless to say that this vendor did not receive an order and we found a different approach to fix the problem.

Whether you would choose to deal with organisations who look at customers as cash cows is another matter.

There are a number of other critical factors in examining whether you really need support

- **The Security Dilemma.** Corporate security teams are becoming ever more sensitive to the risk of intrusion and data loss. Patching and running the latest versions can be compulsory particularly in Financial Services.
- **External facing systems.** Any customer facing systems, such as websites, or those shared with third parties are more vulnerable to attack. Support may again be a necessity with these.

- **Costs of downtime.** Revenue-generating systems lose money if they are down. If a failure is not due to simple infrastructure issue, then vendor support may be the only way to restore a service. If you do not have a contract, you can be open to punitive charges from vendors to provide emergency support.
- **Data protection & Reputational risk.** Organisations have legal responsibilities to protect their customer data. Breaches can have a devastating impact. Reports in the press suggest that "Talk Talk" lost over 100,000 customers after its recent breach.
- **Audit.** Both external and internal auditors are looking ever more closely at how public and major organisations are managing their IT.

Exercise

Take the previous applications and look carefully at the needs of each of these services to determine the impact of them being unavailable.

What are the costs and impact to the organisation?

Compare this to the service costs. Do you feel the service costs are warranted by the potential risks?

5.3. The Enterprise Lifecycle

44

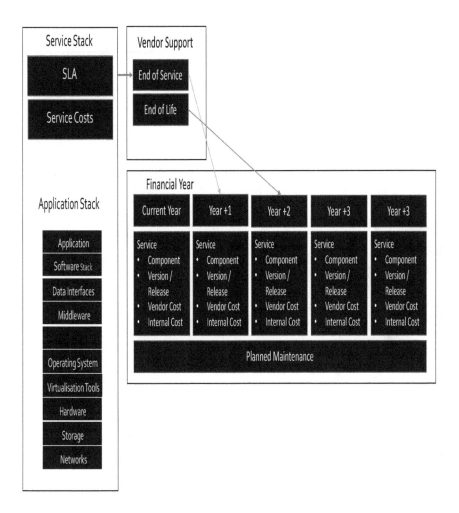

Initially, the discovery phase starts by looking at each application and service in turn. At the enterprise level, we need to look at the overall picture to see the best way to manage all of these.

Taken across a five-year window, a number of services will need upgrading every year.

Effectively, we have to look at these across a number of years and start to schedule the upgrades required. The reason for capturing the EOS and EOL information for each service is that this enables us to build schedules, costs, budgets and resourcing across a 3 to 5-year timeline.

Depending on which maintenance mode is adopted (these are discussed in the following sections), this will determine the work required within each year.

The initial discovery and then the service lifecycle map enable these year-by-year schedules to be built.

Horizontal maintenance

There are many ways in which these components can be managed. The most typical is the **Horizontal Maintenance Model.**

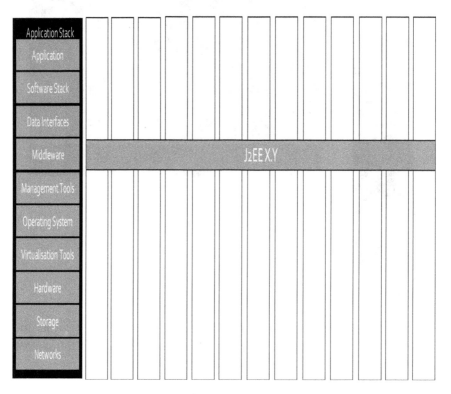

Let's have a look at a typical scenario:

*Say your organisation has 50 different services all
of which use a Java run time environment
(A library which lets Java code run within your environment).*

The security department have advised that there are security concerns about several versions in use and these are also going out of support.

The architects advise that it should be upgraded to a particular version.

You have then been asked to upgrade this as soon as possible.

In principal, this sounds like 50 systems will need to upgraded.

However, a quick sanity check is needed.
Does each of the applications run this version of Java?
Do the vendors support their product on this version of JRE?

In practice, most of the services will work and are supported. However, a number will not.

This is where the fun starts. Do you roll out multiple versions of Java, upgrading to the latest supported version? Are you forced to upgrade the application in order to go the latest version of Java?

Is this covered within a support contract and if not who will pay the upgrade costs? What starts out as an innocuous-sounding request rapidly gets complicated.

The upgrade process ends up as an example of the 80/20 rule. Where 20% of the upgrades take 80% of the effort & cost.

This is how the vast majority of organisations manage their services.

Exercise

See if you can identify a component in the application stack that is used by many applications and is either past the end of support or approaching this.

47

How many instances can you find?

Take a look at a few of these and find out what version of this component that you could upgrade to? Then see if the application vendor supports this particular version?

You may find that the latest version of the component is only supported by a later version of the application which would require an upgrade.

Use an Excel spreadsheet to map out each application version and the last version of the component that it supports. See how many of the applications don't support the latest upgrade. Also, see how many applications need upgrading.

Vertical Maintenance

What if there was a better way?

For every service that is upgraded, testing is required

The most common approach is to perform surface testing and User Acceptance Testing (UAT).

Surface testing is where an IT engineer checks that the application appears to start and is superficially working. They will also check the server and application logs for any error messages.

If everything looks OK, they hand the testing over to the application experts in the form of the application support team and the business subject matter expert to check that the application functionality is working as expected.

So 50 upgrades mean 50 surface tests and UATs.

For each service, every component has an EOS / EOL meaning that there will be many components requiring upgrades each year.

This adds up to a lot of testing, coordinating and change requests!

The chances are that every service has a maximum three-year period where the various components are supported by the respective vendors.

If you have 1000 services, and each of these has 10 component parts, this is a potential 10,000 changes and tests that are likely to be needed across a 3-year period.

In practice, a better way of fixing this is to upgrade the entire service stack to their latest version at the same time.

You then only have to run a single set of tests and the associated change control. If your organisation uses Virtualisation software, it is very straightforward to create a new VM, install all the software and then test. Once it is signed off, then this can be swapped with the live system.

The real benefit is that you now have several years before this needs to be updated again other than for minor patches.

Some real-world examples have shown that this can be 10% of the effort of using the horizontal process.

There are challenges in moving from horizontal to a vertical model. It all hinges on building the lifecycle model and planning what needs to be upgraded and when. There will be a few high-priority items that need to be done first, but then everything becomes much more manageable.

Exercise

Take a look at one of the applications and consider how this would be installed from scratch assuming the current version of the application and the stack.

Also check to see the component versions required by the application.

Estimate how long it would to take to install this and then undertake surface and UAT.

Also look at the vendor's roadmap to see how big a window this would provide before further upgrades are required.

5.4. Summary

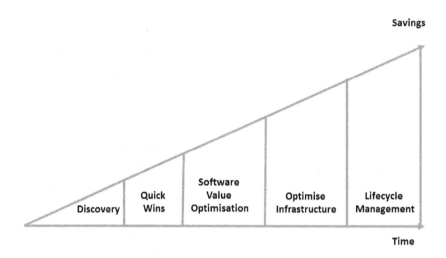

This model shows the whole Software Value Optimisation model merging software with the lifecycles and tools for reducing costs.

Adopting a vertical maintenance model can radically reduce your maintenance costs, improving reliability and supportability. The horizontal model incurs the change management and testing overheads every time a component is upgraded. The vertical approach on the other hand can reduce this by a factor of 4:1 to better.

6

PREDATOR PROTECTION

Purpose: To stop predatory software vendors and bureaucrats from extorting fines as well as additional and unwarranted fees from you.

The risk: Massive unplanned bills with career limiting impact

ROI: Thousands of percent.

"If you swim with Sharks, expect to get eaten."

A recent survey by Flexera reported that 40% of audited Enterprises had been required to pay fees of £70K and 20% of those had to spend in excess of £700K!

*"If there is one area in using software that is a health hazard
to your career and your organisation it is this"*

Failure to understand and act upon this has and does ruin careers.

Key Point

> Let's be straight about this. If your organisation uses more software
> than it is entitled to, then it legally and morally has a duty to pay for
> these additional licences. The Directors or VPs can be personally
> liable and where there has been deliberate abuse then there are
> severe penalties.

Now let's look at the opposite extreme where licencing is used as a tool
to extort additional money from licensees.

According to Gartner, Software Audit requests are rising. 68% of organisations get at least one audit request each year, and what's more, this
figure is climbing. The largest share of requests was said to come from
Microsoft, Oracle, SAP, IBM and Adobe.

If a vendor finds that the organisation is under-licenced, then it can
demand the following:

- Licence fees for the unlicensed software.
- Financial penalties
- The cost of the audit
- Retrospective licences fees from whenever the vendor thinks
  you were under licenced.

These fees can be substantial. I have heard of one business being
presented with a demand approaching £70M.

The software licences that you acquire from a vendor grants you a right
to use their software ad there will be various conditions attached to
this. The vendor is primarily concerned with ensuring that the client is
in compliance with the licence numbers and conditions.

However, an organisation is more concerned with their entitlement to use the software and extract the best possible value from this.

Businesses are by their very nature dynamic: they grow, shrink, acquire and change over time. There are always new employees and leavers. Each of these employees will need access to the right tools and software to perform their role effectively.

This means that the IT teams are constantly responding to starter and leaver requests as well as the need to provide additional software as needed. There is a constant need to be able to flex licencing to reflect this.

Certain licence types allow software to be freely installed without checking that the organisation actually has the corresponding number of licences.

Some vendors such as Microsoft allow an annual or half yearly "true-up" allowing the organisation to temporarily use more licences and then pay any additional fees later. This tends to apply to rental models used by services such as Office 365 or enterprise licencing. This model can work remarkably well for both the vendor and the client. A dedicated licencing server records usage information and this will be checked periodically by the vendor to determine any true-up fees that are due. This can go down, as well as up, so reflects changing business needs.

This model is based upon providing flexibility for the client and in the long run, the vendor probably makes more money by not antagonising their clients

It's fair to say that not every licencing mechanism or vendor works this way. Most are not this flexible, but the key mechanisms used to install the software may allow over-use. Most larger organisations will have enterprise type licences where the vendor provides a master key to allow a single key to install all copies of the software. This reduces the leg work needed where unique keys have to be generated for each installation.

Where a number of people have access to the licence master keys, it is relatively easy to become under licenced.

Key Point

> The flexibility offered by having master keys for software also
> enables the software to be over-installed. This situation rarely
> arose with more traditional key generation schemes. It could be
> assumed that by providing this flexibility, the vendor made it likely
> that this would provide additional opportunities for more income
> and penalty fee revenue.

Enterprise keys can ultimately expose an organisation to a higher risk of audit.

Modern licencing tools are both powerful and effective. It is possible to prevent over-usage. Most software makes use of a feature I like to call "Phone Home". Just like ET, the software likes to report back over the Internet and let the vendor know it has been installed and likely also provide some details as to the surrounding infrastructure.

By providing master keys, coupled with a "Phone Home" mechanism, the vendor has set a nice trap encouraging you to exceed your quota and then knowing when it is time to go and perform an audit to get some extra money from you.

It is alleged that the majority of audits happen because the vendor **knows** that you are under licenced. The reason they know is that the software reports back and it is simple to establish the number of copies in use.

The vendors could stop you from every being under-licenced, but they would be losing out on extra revenues and fees if they did!

Complex terms and conditions

The other trap that can generate unexpected invoices is around the terms and conditions surrounding software. There has been widespread criticism of licencing terms for almost as long as the software industry has existed. The reasons for this go far beyond simple protection of the vendor's intellectual property.

Each country has its own legal systems. Copyright and protection of Intellectual Property exists within Western countries, but these vary considerably. There are often limitations as to the protection offered to both vendors and clients. The vendors often try and increase their protection above and beyond that offered within law. This is often to the detriment of the client and may erode their standard rights.

Some initiatives such as the Transatlantic Trade and Investment Partnership (TTIP) appear to further move the law in favour of the vendor. It goes without saying that any significant software purchase needs specific legal advice to understand the implications. Shrink wrap type terms don't usually appear with enterprise software.

There may be little that can be done about this sort of protection. However, there are many other areas where a little caution can avoid massive bills later.

As well as dealing with intellectual property and your rights to use the software, the contract will also address the infrastructure needed to run the software. There can be a lot of conditions and the complexity of this means that few people bother to read these conditions thoroughly.

Modern technologies such as virtualisation have enabled clients to reduce the running costs of their software by reducing the overall infrastructure costs. In some cases, this also reduces the costs of a vendor's software.

Not surprisingly, the larger vendors have seen this as a threat to their revenue streams and have responded with a variety of approaches to ensure that they maximise their income. Some have responded by only permitting the use of their own virtualisation software or strictly specifying exactly how this can be used.

It is highly likely that a vendor has specified the exact scenarios in which their software can be used, but also made it difficult to be sure that you are 100% compliant. It is rare to see a plain English, simple licencing statement. Some require both legal and technical expertise to properly interpret and most organisations do not go to these lengths to ensure that they understand their entitlement and obligations.

Audits are increasingly being used as a sales and negotiating tool to increase revenues. InfoWorld reported an ex-Oracle executive saying that "An Audit was used to find some issues, put some fear into their hearts and throw up a big number. Then you close a deal on something else they want to buy in order to make the audit issues go away".

Recently, giant confectioner Mars Inc. filed a lawsuit against Oracle. It accused the vendor of using "Out-of-scope" licencing enforcement based upon "False premises". The suit was settled out of court and the terms of the deal have not been published. You can draw your own conclusions from this.

This complexity ensures that you are more likely to breach the terms and conditions of a software contract. This in turn provides more opportunities for the vendor to make more money.

There are some common scenarios that need to be handled with care:

Disaster Recovery (DR), test & development.

For all except the most critical systems, it is not cost-effective to provide completely redundant systems across sites. Some database products are very expensive. Most vendors will provide an option for single licences to be used for the production site and DR site so long as both copies are not running in production at the same time. If a warm or cold cutover happens there should be no risk of this happening.

The use of the same software for testing and development can be much less clear. Often the vendor expects that a copy of the software is purchased for each of these environments. Given the already high costs of some products this is simply too expensive and many organisations do not have separate test and development environments.

Virtualisation and VMs have made it much easier to create inexpensive virtual servers to allow test and development. However, the same is not true for the software. The vendors T&Cs need to be carefully checked to ensure that this is permitted. If not, then additional licences are required.

Upgrades and varying T&C's

Another scenario is that new versions and releases can vary their T&Cs. This applies particularly to shrink-wrap software where by simply opening the package or installing the software you are deemed to have accepted the T&Cs. Do you know anyone who regularly does this?

The situation is generally better with enterprise agreements as changes should be notified, reviewed and agreed by both parties. This makes it far more likely that the contract will have been reviewed.

Supporting documents

Another tactic is to provide other documents that become part of the contract. These can be called many things from addendums to the release notes with the software. However, they would normally be supplied with the media or printed documentation supplied by the vendor.

It is highly dubious if these extra items can legally vary a contract, but needless to say, this has not stopped vendors. A number of these cases have been settled out of court suggesting that the vendor was not keen on the court finding against them and setting a precedent which other cases would then be judged against.

Prerequisites

Some vendors require the installation of additional tools in order to ensure that their software is used correctly. However, this rarely seems to happen in practice. It may simply be that it is not particularly obvious and gets missed. However, some vendors will not allow the use of virtualisation without specific tools in place.

Some licencing models allow the user of the software with capacity limits such as CPU sizes and processing capacity. With virtualisation you can run a number of smaller instances up to the licenced limits. This is measured with a proprietary discovery tool. If you do not have this installed, you can be billed for each instance that you are running, potentially increasing your costs by a factor of 10 or more!

Right to Use (RTU)

Another trap for the unwary is the use of cloud, outsourcing and third-party support services. The licence typically grants your organisation the rights to use this software for your staff within your own IT facilities.

If you outsource your data centres or servers, then you may be in breach of these conditions. Effectively you need an RTU for the outsourcer to manage the software on your behalf or indeed to run it on their servers.

It tends to only be the larger vendors who are aware of the scenarios and most smaller vendors do not have such clauses in their contracts. It is not expensive to arrange RTU's for other parties, but is frequently overlooked.

Similar arrangements are needed for application management suppliers who may also need explicit authorisation to manage your software.

Cloud services can fall into this scenario as well. It is a fairly new consideration and many vendors have not yet had to deal with this situation. However, most commodity cloud hosting is a shared environment and may require an RTU. A private hosting environment probably does not.

Be very wary with cloud hosting, especially when moving between the two environments, as it is possible that you will exceed your licence entitlement during the transition period when there may be users live in both environments. Tackling this upfront with the appropriate vendors can save aggravation and subsequent bills.

Protection strategies

Here are a few tips to help protect your organisation from the more aggressive licencing tactics.

Key Vendor Focus

The first test is simple. Do you run software from the big 5?

Microsoft, IBM, SAP, Oracle, Adobe.

If you do, then the chances are that you will be subject to at least one audit per year from them. If they do audit you, the chances are that they suspect that you are under-licenced.

Key Point

> **IF YOU HAVE SOFTWARE FROM THESE VENDORS THEN YOU HAVE TO ENSURE THAT YOU HAVE CERTANTITY AROUND YOUR COMPLIANCE**

Discovery

The only reliable way to prove compliance, day to day, is through deploying automated discovery tools so that you always have a clear picture of the software in use within your organisation.

Just knowing what is installed is only the starting point. You also have to reconcile this against the licences that you have purchased. The software asset management system will let your record and report on any non-compliance.

Contract Vault

It is one thing knowing what software you have. The opposite side of the coin is that you need to have the contracts and T&C's for these. Having to find these during an audit is going to cause a lot of stress and questions from senior management.

It is a good idea to create an online vault or store where electronic copies are kept alongside scans of paper based documents.

Licencing Team

Software licencing has grown to the point where it requires a team of people to manage it effectively. The liabilities and penalties more than justify this. Indeed, done properly, there is a massive ROI from this.

For medium to large organisations there are a number of team roles

- **Software procurement specialist.** They are responsible for negotiating the best possible deal and liaising directly with the vendors. They normally are involved with the initial purchase and renewals.
- **Software contract specialist (or third party licencing solicitors).** Any significant software contract needs to be reviewed by a specialist solicitor to advise on the rights, obligations and implications of the contract. For smaller organisations, this role can be undertaken by an external legal practice with the appropriate skills.
- **Solution or software Architect.** They determine the IT environment and how the licencing restrictions impact these. They should also be responsible for checking that any vendor prerequisites are met. They are often the only persons who can interpret these requirements and document them in the BAU operational documentation for the service.
- **Licencing manager.** Their role is to own the overall process and lifecycle, ensuring that upcoming renewals are forecast and appropriate steps are in place to negotiate renewals.
- **Software administrator.** This person keeps track of the licences, deployments and reports. They will liaise with the manager and maintain compliance records. They will need to be trained in the Software Asset Management System.

With the exception of the administrator, these roles don't have to be full-time.

Vendor tools & prerequisites

Before any software is installed, the contract, documentation and FAQs **MUST** be checked to see if there is any other software that you need to install. Alternatively, there may be restrictions over exactly how you can use the software with virtualisation for instance.

I have seen organisations that build checklists for every software application. These go through a wide range of areas that must be checked and recorded before the software can be used. The service documentation often contains installation workbooks reminding anyone who installs the software of what must be done. Generally, a solutions architect reviews the vendor documentation and produces these workbooks.

Dealing with gaps

If gaps are found, these must be addressed immediately. There are three options: remove the software, obtain additional licences or do both of these. There should be policies that specify what to do in these circumstances.

The longer the period of time that software is unlicensed, the more chance you have of an audit and the larger the potential penalty.

Carrot & Stick

Knowing that major vendors use audits as a sales tool to get more money from you presents an opportunity to make this work to your advantage.

Do you know how your software vendor's sales team is incentivised? They expect to earn huge bonuses, but if they don't meet their quarterly sales target, they are thrown out. When a salesperson gets desperate they are far more likely to resort to audits to generate sales, even though it will ruin the client relationship. Better than getting the sack....

A number of years ago, I was at the offices of a well-known vendor who had a video wall and presentation running in the canteen area. As we ate lunch, it was praising their high performers and how far they were over target. Then came the surprise, 3 unfortunates were mentioned who were underperforming. The gist of this was clear – they were on their way out if they didn't improve. It was uncomfortable to watch as a customer, yet alone for the sales person!

This is a real story and shows the degree of pressure being exerted on their sales teams to perform.

The migration to cloud services directly threatens many of these vendors as you are less likely to need their licences. Audits can be used as a short-term tool to extract more money, but this can be counterproductive.

Being stung by an aggressive vendor makes you far more likely to throw them out.

Vendors are increasingly looking to encourage existing clients to migrate to their own cloud services and have been known to use the audit to this end. As has been reported, they kick off an audit, set in the fear, throw around some frightening figures and then offer a cloud service as a way to avoid this.

However, these cloud deals are often on better terms than you may have been offered directly. If you are threatened with an audit, it makes sense to dangle to the sales person that you are thinking about going to their cloud. It can be used to get better prices.

Beware the Trojan Horse

Some of the bigger vendors often pay lip service to your concerns about needing to reduce your maintenance costs. They may well offer a free service to see if they can help reduce your costs. This touchy feely helpful account manager is nothing of the sort. It is a way of running a disguised audit and giving the vendor a chance to bill you for more money.

This is similar to the free "Winter Check" offered by your car dealer, where you can guarantee that something will be found that needs to be "fixed".

Always turn down any free offer of this sort.

Lockdown

If you are running Thin Client devices, it is possible to restrict the number of software licences in use and indeed stop anyone else installing the software. Citrix, terminal services and VMware's VDI tools are widely used to build and manage applications and virtual desktops. Every desktop needs to have a signed and approved change request before it is created. It is also possible to restrict the number of applications deployed and concurrent user numbers.

These tools enable enforcement of your licences and make it very difficult for these numbers to be exceeded.

Restrict keys

Licence keys, access to media and licencing portals need to be ruthlessly controlled. Failure to do so results in proliferation and massive under-licencing risks.

The licencing manager and administrator should be the only people who grant access to the media and keys.

Employment contracts and penalties

Your employment contracts should include conditions that employees may not install their own software and also are responsible for company software. Abuse of this is a disciplinary offence and should be communicated as such. Although vendors won't allow employee misuse of the software as a valid excuse to let an organisation off, it is still a good tool to stop abuse in the first place.

Packaging

In order to install software, a user needs to have admin rights to their PC. However, few people have a legitimate need for these elevated rights.

Good practice is to restrict this as much as possible and maintain audit logs.

Modern tools such as Microsoft's AppV (Application Virtualisation) can be used to create packages which consist of an application and all of the components that it needs to run. This package can then be deployed to laptops, PCs, servers and virtual desktops automatically via tools such as Microsoft's System Centre Configuration Manager (SCCM). These admin tools and processes have the appropriate rights to install or upgrade software, but the user does not. This can effectively stop licencing breaches via end-users.

Software Asset Management

Asset management tools are not optional. They are the only tool that can identify non-compliance in near real-time and let you address this before it becomes an issue with a vendor.

This is a proactive measure that detects non-compliance and alerts the licencing team so this can be dealt with immediately.

Exercise

Create a quick strawman to see how many of these areas are covered or exposed.

Look at the following areas:

Software Media
Software Keys
HR Policies
Tools & Reporting
Responsibilities
Budget

Start with the key vendors and see if you work with vendors who are likely to audit regularly.

Legislation and Compliance

Identity fraud has become an ever more serious issue in almost every country and there are many instances of this being linked to personal information being stolen from companies.

Regulators are finally waking up to the risks that information theft poses and starting to do something about this. The UK has had the Data Protection Act for many years, but ultimately the fines and the reputational damage from a very public data breach have already damaged some very large organisations such as Sony.

The European Union is introducing the General Data Protection Regulation (GDPR) to regulate and standardise the treatment of personal data across the whole of this area.

It is also introducing very serious penalties for data breaches, significant enough to make any organisation take note. The penalties range up to 4% of global turnover or 20m Euros, depending on which is greater.

The legislation also covers European data being processed outside of the EU.

Sony and Talk Talk were both very lucky that this legislation was not in force at the time that they had their lapses! In addition to losing customers, they would now receive very substantial fines.

GDPR will require formal classification of data, the implementation of appropriate controls and external verification of an organisation's compliance.

It is fair to say that much of this is best practice and would be expected of reputable organisations, but GDPR will now enforce this and give it real teeth.

The legislation is not necessarily onerous to implement. However, given the cost of not complying, the implementation cost is a drop in the ocean.

Some countries also have Freedom of Information (FOI)-type legislation. This needs appropriate management controls. There again are penalties around this, but they are nowhere near as substantial as GDPR.

7

PUTTING IT ALL TOGETHER...
INSIDER TIPS

*Although each of these steps are effective in finding ways
to reduce your costs, their real power comes from
the synergy when all of the steps are applied together.*

Each of these six steps are interlinked. This can become a process where you need to loop two or three times to get the best answers. This is actually a good thing and shows that the intricacies of the environment, requirements and software are becoming better understood.

KEY TIP - Don't get too bogged down in detail.

If your organisation has a lot of software packages, it can appear fairly daunting to complete the discovery phase and evaluate how to save money.

In practice, the best returns often come from a very small subset of the software.

It's a bit like the 80/20 rule. However, I have often found with software it's more like 90/10 or even 95/5.

5% of your software will yield the best savings for the least effort.

KEY TIP - Get an asset management package.

Over a number of years, I have seen many different ways of determining which software is in use.

This can range from sending out questionnaires, reviewing purchase orders and invoices through to teams looking at every PC and automated tools.

Software complexity has evolved to the point where manual audits are ineffective and can create a false sense of security.

Relying on manual methods is time consuming, expensive, error prone and can massively underreport on what is really being used.

If you get audited by a vendor or a third-party, they will almost always use tools and it puts you in a very vulnerable position if your discovery is not as thorough as the vendor's. After all they have a vested interest in tripping you up.

Software licencing is normally driven by the fear that you will be found to be non-compliant and a vendor may be seeking substantial extra sums of money that you don't have.

Automating this process puts your organisation in the driving seat. The focus can then return to getting the best out of your software and min-imising the costs.

7.1. Application Delivery Models

Cloud computing provides ways of deploying software as an alternative to the traditional self-hosted or outsourcer hosting models.

These allow you to rent servers in a datacentre which is accessed via the Internet. The costing models charge based upon provision and usage depending on the package chosen. Importantly, they also allow servers to be dynamically scalable so that performance can be altered in line with business demand.

Let's have a look at the different models.

7.2. Infrastructure as a Service (IAAS)

With IAAS, the vendor provides the Virtual Machines (VMs). This consists of the datacentre network and storage, physical hardware and the virtualisation software.

From a support perspective, they support only these components. There will also be an interface to enable you to manage the VMs. This normally includes some reporting and billing summary information. You are responsible for everything else. This means your service desk needs to log support calls, application support, vendor liaison and Wintel support for everything above the VMs.

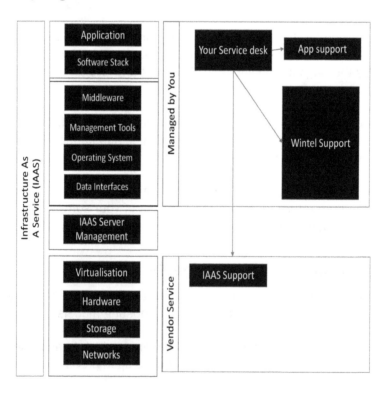

7.3. Platform as a Service (PAAS)

With PAAS, the vendor provides an IAAS layer and everything below the software stack. The Operating System, Management tools such as Anti-Virus, Middleware and interfaces to databases are included.

The vendor provides at least first-line support for these. You are responsible for the application and the software stack needed to run the application. This means you provide the service desk to log support calls, provide first-line application support and liaise with the application vendor where appropriate.

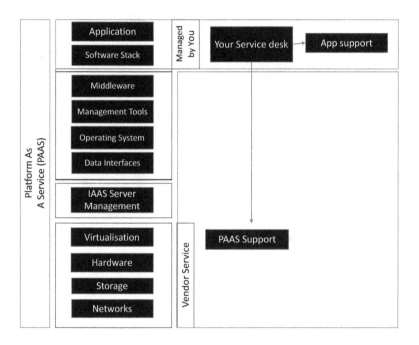

7.4. Software as a Service (SAAS)

This is where a vendor provides the entire service including hardware, software and the support. The application is accessed through a web browser via the Web or a VPN connection.

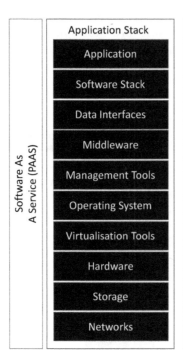

The charging mechanism can vary depending on the type of application and the value of the service.

Some great examples of SAAS products are:

- **Salesforce.Com** – Customer relationship management.
- **Office 365** – Email, collaboration, Microsoft Office and web hosting
- **Xero** – An online accounting package that lets you run your finances from the net.
- **Microsoft Azure / Amazon Web Services** – Cloud hosted virtual servers and associated virtual infrastructure.

Pricing tends to be per user providing certainty about costs. These services are also scalable so that adding additional storage or users is straightforward and as simple as completing an online form. It is also possible to simply reduce the resources and costs.

7.5. Potential Cost Savings

The theme of this book is reducing the costs of running applications and services.

These different models offer useful options to reduce the costs of in-house servers and the associated service wrappers around these.

It is also possible to use VMware and competing tools to virtualise in house. Until recently, this was the main approach to virtualisation.

The cost savings of virtualisation are not always as clear-cut as vendors would like.

The cost of the virtualisation software was roughly the same cost as the VM Host server.

As a rule of thumb, a virtual host server (basically a powerful physical server with a lot of memory and fast IO) would cost £10,000. However, the VMware costs for this were broadly similar. Depending on the workload of the VMs to be run on this host, it would typically support between 5 and 20 VMs.

I have seen may cost cases where the VMware costs had been left out and this literally made the ROI look 50% better than it really was.

So a host would replace between 5 and 20 physical servers. Depending on your internal cost per server, this is a significant cost saving.

Now if you look at Cloud, the equation really starts to change. I suspect that some of the vendors such as Microsoft and Amazon are seriously discounting their virtualisation software if not including it free to win business. They can be as much as 50% cheaper if not more over an in-house solution.

These savings are hard to ignore.

The service management costs can also reduce with Cloud solutions.

Service Integration and management (SIAM) is an emerging area which attempts to automate many of the overheads of managing these services. Tools such as Service Now include integration to these Cloud services and even can automate the provisioning of Cloud services and the associated credentials.

There are many benefits to Cloud-based services

- Elasticity to scale as required
- Business Continuity
- Software updates
- Revenue not capital expenditure
- Easier collaboration
- Work from anywhere with an internet connection
- Centralised information / reduction in data loss
- Provides small business with Enterprise-level tools
- Scalable

Exercise

Using the same applications from the previous exercise, think through which of these Cloud models may be suitable.

Would it be better to migrate the application to an IAAS or PAAS model? Alternatively do the application vendors offer this as a SAAS model?

Also consider how much data is used and how this could be moved to a cloud service?

7.6. Low Hanging Fruit

A number of server uses are well suited to moving to IAAS and PAAS platforms.

- **Lightly used servers.** These have always been ideal candidates for virtualisation. The same applies for Cloud. The virtualisation tools enable these to be moved quickly to the Cloud. Each VM is then given a resource profile to match its needs. In this case, the more basic plans should be more than adequate.

- **Test & development environments.** Test & Dev tends to only be used when a new version or new release needs checking and can benefit from a small VM. Currently, these start from around £10 per month which is far cheaper than using a physical server. Some services can also be stopped when not in use, reducing the billing to a minimum.
- **Database servers.** This is one area that can work out radically cheaper. Taking Microsoft's SQL Server, it is possible to build resilient services using Azure more cheaply than it can be done in-house. Many firms are forced to move to Enterprise server to build resilient services. However, using VMs, it is possible to get similar levels of service using standard edition VMs. These are also scalable to 16 cores. Most of the time you can bypass the need for Enterprise and save around £20K per instance.
- **Data warehousing.** Building data cubes in-house is expensive due to the cost of the licences and server power that is needed. This is another area where the cloud offerings are considerably cheaper.

One caveat is that some scenarios require the application, servers and databases to be located within the same cloud. Otherwise, you are looking to move data over the Internet which is a significant bottleneck.

You may even want to look at an organisational tenancy where all of the VMs are with a single vendor and logically connected via the network within the cloud datacentre to maximise performance and provide effective security.

7.7. The Downsides of Cloud Computing

The glossy web pages and brochures all promote Cloud computing as the best thing since sliced bread. In reality, they skim over the fact that additional investment is needed to facilitate the transition from in-house to Cloud. In addition, service models change considerably. For those used to outsourcers who handle almost everything, there is a lot more that either has to be done in-house to manage the service or you need to use third party services and tools to simplify this.

Cloud computing needs to have some form of identity management that enables single sign-on between different servers and services. This is often an extension of Microsoft's Active Directory service.

Where there are multiple SAAS services in use, Identity Management (IDM) is essential. Otherwise your users will end up having to have different credentials for each of these services. IDM allows a common ID and password to be used for everything.

IDM is still in its infancy and most larger organisations seem to buy in third-party tools to facilitate this. There is a cost associated with this and it can be substantial. In addition, connectivity also needs to be considered. Existing Internet connections may have the bandwidth to run a few applications, but for large-scale use, dedicated connections are likely to be needed along with resilience.

Whilst Cloud Computing costs look very attractive, these extra costs need to be considered as a part of the overall costs.

Effectively there is a critical mass of servers which makes the transition to Cloud worthwhile. If these numbers make sense, then there is the potential to save considerable sums of money as well as outsourcing a lot of the current headaches.

The other factor that needs to be considered is the cost of transition.

There are steps needed to move your servers from your current hosting to cloud hosting.

At a high level the process looks like this:

- Physical servers need to be virtualised via a Physical 2 Virtual (P2V) process. This has also been dubbed Physical to Cloud (P2C). This creates a VM which is an image representing the memory map of the original server.
- The network details such as IP addresses need to be updated to reflect the configuration of the new hosting environment.
- Data and databases either need to be ported or the access paths need to be updated.
- Management tools need to be added or reconfigured.
- Everything needs to be tested and signed off.

- Documentation needs to be updated to reflect revised configurations.
- DR arrangements need to be tested.
- The majority of these steps also need to be managed via change control with an appropriate approval process.

These steps are not insignificant and need to be costed.

An IT Director I worked with went to a Microsoft event about their Azure-based cloud offerings. When he returned, he decided that we needed to migrate as soon as possible because some of the servers cost £6 per month as opposed to the £120 we were paying our existing provider. We had a problem affording test and development environments and this appeared to offer an affordable alternative.

Taken in isolation, it looks a lot cheaper. However, the Microsoft offering was effective IAAS whereas the existing servers were provided on a PAAS model.

In order to move to Cloud, a new Identity Management system was required and there are costs to virtualise and configure the servers. It can easily cost £1000 just to move a single server. However, costs can be reduced by moving several related servers together.

The key message is to make sure that you compare a 5-year cost of ownership model against these transition costs.

Most of the time virtualisation and Cloud migration saves money, but not always.

7.8. Summary

Cloud computing makes a lot of sense and in the right circumstances can save a lot of money.

There is a critical mass of services that makes the transition costs worthwhile. The cost savings achieved by using the Cloud need to exceed the current running costs AND the transition costs.

By carefully working through these costs, it is possible to find the breakeven points where Cloud makes sense.

8

THE ULTIMATE GOAL —
BUILD YOUR INFRASTRUCTURE TO
MINIMISE YOU LICENSE COSTS

A common theme is that we inherit the infrastructure in our organisation and this drives how we can deploy software which in turn determines the costs of the software licences and services.

Strategically it is possible to architecture your infrastructure so that it reduces software costs.

Economies of scales — SAAS

Adding physical infrastructure is costly and often slow. There are many considerations and delays. Servers, OS, cables, rack space, power, air conditioning, lead times, purchase orders, change controls and resources are all needed.

Cloud hosted infrastructure is a different matter. It can be as straight-forward as selecting the most appropriate server offering, entering your credit card details and then clicking confirm. The virtual provisioning will then spin a server up for you in a matter of hours.

Virtual infrastructure also lets you design for average rather than peak workloads. In your own data centre particularly with physical servers, you have to design for the peak load and when these servers are underutilised you are paying for that investment.

However, many of the cloud services and virtualisation tools let you dynamically scale your VMs automatically or manually. At year end, you can double the amount of horse power. You just get a bigger bill in the following month.

SANs have similar features where they can auto-tier your storage to provide the most appropriate type for an application. The various cloud vendors are already offering services that offer scaling and auto-tiering. It is a great way to minimise costs and then boost performance when you most need this.

Below average utilisation is an indicator as to whether you should buy or rent licences as well as whether SAAS would be a better option.

Capital vs Revenue Costs

Cash-strapped organisations often look for revenue-based models which let them pay for their services with small recurring fees rather than having to pay large lump sums.

Cash-rich organisations tend to purchase software outright and find it easier to fund large capital outlays.

Until recently, the IT industry tended to operate on a capital basis with high initial purchase costs and lower annual maintenance and support costs.

The advent of SAAS has made it much easier to move to a revenue-based model reducing running costs as well as making it easier to scale or shrink as needed.

These steps work together to help you get the lowest operating cost for your services.

The utilisation figures often show opportunities for selecting different licence types which may suit your organisation better.

A simple change to the infrastructure can reduce the number of physical servers needed

Cloud lock in.

There is a saying that everything in life is a compromise. Cloud has its good and bad points.

With IT, the cost of ownership is the key to determining how best to deploy software. Understanding the different stacks and scenarios provides guidance as to which option is best.

Cloud moves from large initial payments to smaller regular payments. Whilst this is a good thing for cash-strapped businesses, it is also a lock in as these payments continue for as long as you use the service. It can make it harder to return to paying up front in the future.

Migration away from cloud is also difficult. Rebuilding an in-house data centre is very expensive and time consuming. It has been difficult to move between outsourcers and the challenges around this are well understood. However, cloud-to-cloud migration lacks standards and is likely to have plenty of pitfalls.

On the positive side, this should get easier over time as tools and standards emerge.

So long as you are aware of these pitfalls and have done you planning you are OK.

It's worth being aware of the risk of exchange rates going against your favour. Many services are priced in dollars and weakening exchange rates mean that your costs could rise.

Try and get pricing in your native currency. If you are converting from dollars to other currencies, there can be major risks around future fluctuations.

The pound to dollar in the 1980s moved from £1.50 to £2.25 in a very short space of time. For car exporters this increased the price of their products very quickly and rapidly made them unattractive in dollar-priced markets.

Imagine if your new cloud service became 33% more expensive over 6 months. This derails all of your calculations. Native pricing protects you.

Also look at the vendor's right to increase prices annually. Make sure that there is some cap against this.

8.1. Summary

Virtual infrastructure offers elasticity and the ability to quickly scale your resources to meet the changing needs of the business.

It also offers tools to minimise database and application costs. By virtually building the right infrastructure, it becomes possible to utilise the cheapest licence models and have the flexibility to adapt.

9

TIPS FOR SUCCESS

Use the SVO Scorecard

The Software Value Optimisation scorecard can quickly help to determine your potential for saving money.

This report can help to identify weaknesses and justify the effort to your management.

This can be found at:
http://softwarevalueoptimisation.com/software-scorecard-2/

Information overload is the biggest single challenge when looking to reduce software costs. Most organisations have hundreds if not thousands of applications.

If you start trying to work through the details of every application, you are going to struggle.

I have always been an advocate of Pareto's Principle - better known as the 80/20 rule. This rule says that 80 % of the results come from 20% of the effort. Why focus on the 20% that takes 80% of the effort?

This very much applies to identifying the applications which will yield the best savings. There are two simple measures that help:

- **The number of licences in use.** A cheap piece of software used by a handful of people is not worth the effort to see if you can reduce its costs. However, if it is used by everyone in your organisation, it is likely to be worth exploring further.
- **The most expensive applications.** Expensive software should always be reviewed. It is often the quickest way to realise savings.

Using asset management tools is always the easiest way to accurately determine the applications in use. The starting point is to get these tools deployed to every PC and server. Over a week or so, the asset databases are then constructed and available for reporting.

I normally look for a summary report that will show you the applications sorted by the number of licences. This quickly shows the low-hanging fruit worthy of further investigation.

The next step is to import this information into Excel.

The reason for doing this is that asset management systems rarely record or report the value of the licences. In Excel, add columns for the licence costs, total cost (licences times cost) and a target column to flag the applications worth your time and effort.

Some of the applications will be known to you and they will come across as being great candidates. Others may need a quick Google search to find their purpose and rough pricing.

QUICK TIP

Searching for a product name followed by "price" indicates to Google that you are interested in purchasing the item and it will often bring up price comparison sites. These let you quickly see the average prices which can then be added to your spreadsheet.

It is always worth finding out these average prices and adding them to your spreadsheet. It gives you proof that reducing the number of licences will save substantial sums of money and this can be used for business cases or even as evidence in appraisals of your contribution to the organisation.

Once you have this information together, you have your plan of action. Completing this spreadsheet rarely takes more than a matter of hours.

This is a critical first step and is incredibly motivating!

10
FREE TIPS.......

Sign up to our newsletter to get expert tips at
http://Softwarevalueoptimisation.com

11
WHAT TO DO NEXT?

Optimising your environment to save money is a journey consisting of 4 specific stages.

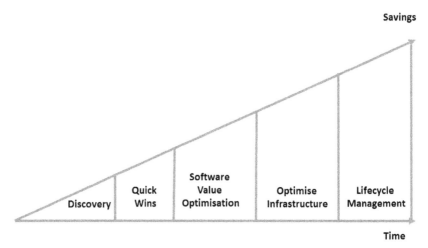

There are a number of tools that we offer to help you progress faster through this journey.

The Software Value Optimisation Scorecard. This is a tool to understand the maturity of your organisation and identify the potential for both unexpected costs and the potential to reduce overall costs.

This can be accessed at our website,
    http://softwarevalueoptimisation.com/software-scorecard-2/

The Savings Accelerator. This is an intense programme designed to train an organisation to realise these savings.

SVO Mentoring Programme. This is a mentoring process to help internal teams through this journey and provide accountability and assistance with the various challenges that may arise.

12
THE AUTHOR

Steve Butler is an author, speaker, IT consultant and entrepreneur based in Stratford Upon Avon, England.

Steve runs a number of business including an IT consultancy specialising in reducing IT costs and a business that publishes books on treating common joint problems.

Steve is also a speaker for a range of IT events and webinars. He has won quality and innovation awards from major organisations such as IBM.

His interests include cycling, martial arts and alternative health.

www.ingramcontent.com/pod-product-compliance
Lightning Source LLC
Chambersburg PA
CBHW070849070326
40690CB00009B/1765